Dooms Day Prepping 101
Written By: Chris Wilson

Special Thanks

When writing this guide I kept thinking about a lot of people, such as Alex Jones for opening my eyes to whats going on in the world, and to all the troops that have to "bug out" on a daily basis being stationed in other countries defending our country while it's being attacked from the inside. I also thought about my grandfather who taught me how to live off of the land by growing my own food. May you rest in peace Robert White.

A lot of other topics also popped into my head that has to do with "Doomsday Prepping" like does people really have the money to make prep, and will people really take whats being said seriously, which I hope you do. Because no matter what the doomsday is you should always be prepared.

If you would like to see more from me check out www.cyanide-news.com
If you would like to check out the news side of things you can check out www.infowars.com

Also make sure to check us out on facebook at www.facebook.com/cyanidenewsnetwork and on twitter at www.twitter.com/cyanidenewsnet

We are a proud supporter of Wise Food Products so if you looking for some great food at a low price make sure to check out www.wisefoodstorage.com

Prologue

Prepping for the worst can mean many different things depending upon who you ask, but in the end, its still dooms day. It might not be a world wide, nation wide, state wide, or even city wide dooms day, but it is dooms day for that person. This book will inform you on how to cover all disasters, may it be personal, or natural disaster. We will cover natural disasters such as.

- Flood
- Fires
- Tornadoes
- Hurricanes
- Earthquakes

We will also cover why you should stock up now because of

- Job Loss
- Power Outages (due to storms and rolling brown outs)

We will be covering short term prepping and long term prepping when covering this we will cover

- Food
- Water
- Emergency Tools

By the time you are done reading this book you will know

1. Why you should prep
2. What you should prep
3. What a B.o.B is
4. How to protect your materials
5. Strategic Relocation
6. and finally why all this is important

Reasons To Prep

So prepping has your attention or you wouldn't have the book, so you are wondering what do I have to do to make sure I am able to survive on my own if anything ever happens. Well you have came to the right place. The first thing we will be covering is WHY you should prep!

There are many reasons to prep, one reason is just to know your safe no matter what happens, having that confidence that you are gonna survive if
1. You lose your job
2. A bad storm knocks the electric out
3. Tornado's hit your area
4. If you live in a hurricane area
5. If you live in an area that prone to earthquakes
6. If we have rolling black outs due to more power being used then what the transformers can handle
7. and many more reasons

Losing Your Job
You got a great job now, just finished paying off your house so you own it out right, but with the way the economy is who knows if you will have you job tomorrow? Why not make sure that you are prepared for the worst instead of having to wait to find a new job or waiting for your unemployment to kick in? You should stock up on the things you absolutely need in case you lose your job because if you lose your job and you have to wait, you could go hungry, go thirsty be without electric because you don't have the money to pay for everything, why put yourself through that when you can take care of it today?

Storms Tornado's and Hurricanes Knocks Out Electric

It's summer time and we all know how the weather is, pop up severe storms popping up everywhere and a storm hits your area and the electric goes out, you live in a big city or out in the country either way you know it takes forever for the power companies to get the power back on. During this time your food in the refrigerator goes bad, you have nothing to eat because all you have is canned food but no way of opening it because you got rid of that hand crank can opener years ago. You head to the store and find out that there's hundreds if not thousands of people there or have already been there to buy food as well and there is little to nothing left.

Earthquakes

An earthquake hits your area splitting roads, opening up sink holes destroying a lot of stuff around you is destroyed. Your electrics out, but whats that matter because it's not safe to stay in. You get in your car and find out that you can't move it because the road is to bad behind you so you have to go by foot. It's hot and dry outside you know you need food and water but you know if you carry around food that you have in the fridge that it will spoil and wear you out faster.

With all this being said, what can you do? Prep, that's what you do. By the time you finish reading this book you will know exactly what to do. First off before you buy anything you need to come up with a budget (all budgets are different and there is something out there for everyone so don't worry if you just make minimum wage).

Starting out you just want to get enough stuff to last you and your family three days, then build from there.

Where To Start?

Like was mentioned at the end of the last section, start off with a seventy-two hour food and water supply for you and your family. You can get long shelf life food anywhere on the internet but there are a few that I suggest you use, because they have the best food, they are the cheapest and the most reliable. (find list at the end of the guide). In the food selection that you get, you want to make sure that you get three breakfast's three lunches and three dinners per person. You also want to make sure that you have water stored so that you can stay hydrated, I do not suggest you buy bottled water because it has been known to go bad (yea water goes bad when in BPA coated plastic) the sites that I list have different size jugs and water bags that you can store water in, I will also list a link to where you can get your own water purification systems in case you have to drink un-purified water.

Once you get your three days worth of food, you will want to check into getting some kind of power generator that won't cost you anything to run, meaning solar generators, windmills, hand crank generators (for small devices just to make sure you have a way to communicate). You will also want to get a first aid kit unless you already have one, the reason you need this is because if the electric is out, or an earthquake has happened on any natural disaster, the city water system wont be safe to use because it has not been treated (not saying that it's safe when it is but that's another story). With the first-aid kit you will be able to take care of small cuts and scraps so that they don't get infected.

So you got your 72 hours worth of food, now what?

So you have gotten your seventy-two hours worth of food and water, your generator and your first aid kit and you still want to prep? If you get this taken care of and you still want to prep to make sure you and your family is OK no matter what happens. Start buying more food (making sure you have a place to store it) because there is nothing worse then having to much stuff that you can't find what your looking for. Get a water proof, durable decent sized back pack/tactical bag and take the seventy-two hour food supply, the water, the generator and first aid kit and put it in the bag, making sure that you have everything fixed so that you don't have to take everything out to get something out that you are going to be using all the time. At this time you will want to make sure to get a solar blanket, a tube tent, a portable cooking stove (with spare heating discs), a compass, and some sort of knife (depends upon what kind of knife you prefer) you will also want to get hand sanitizer and a pack of cards (your choice of what kind) for some kind of entertainment. This is called your Bug out Bag, or B.o.B the reason for this will be explained later on.

Now back to stocking up on storable food at the place you live for long term food.   When stocking up on food for your long term food supply it is cheaper to buy it in bulk meaning either by the month or by the three month supply or higher because they do make it up to a year supply, the companies give you some great discounts, plus they usually through in extra food so that it gives you more each time. If you can't afford this no problem just get what you can, I'm picky so I personally buy individual pouches and packets so that I know what

I am getting every time I order something.

At this time you might want to check with your city to see if it is OK to have a small garden and or a green house so that you can grow your own produce through out the year. By doing this you will have fresh produce year round which will save you a lot of money through out time in two ways, you won't have to buy canned food anymore and you will be able to be a little more selective upon what you order in your long term food storage because you will be able to can your own produce to have it around.

Bug Out Bag

The bag that you have the seventy-two hours worth of food, water and all the other materials is called a bug out bag, or a B.o.B for short. This is the bag you grab if you ever have to book it out of your house or apartment. The reasons you would leave is if:

- if a pandemic breaks out (air borne virus's, disease)
- your house catches fire (an obvious)
- natural disasters
- car wrecks (your in the car wreck)
- your car breaks down on the side of the road

Having this bug out bag can help you no matter what the problem is because u will have shelter, food, water, heat, a way to protect yourself and entertainment just like at your home. Make sure you replace everything that you use in this bag because you never know when your going to need it again.

When picking a bag to use as your B.o.B make sure that it can hold everything, make sure that it is durable, make sure that it is water proof, and to make things easier on you if you have to use it make sure that it has a pocket on each side so that you can stick a couple things of water in it so you can easily grab it if you get thirsty. Keep this bag at the location you spend most of your time at, and if you work more then a mile away from where you live it wouldn't hurt to have another one with the same exact stuff as the first one at the place you work.

How To Protect Your Stockpile

You now have your stockpile of food and water built up for long term disasters, now you have to protect it in case anything happens and people try to loot. There are many ways of doing this from the simplest form of buying a gun, and registering it (wink wink), all the way up to getting a surveillance system to be able to view who is around your property (if you rent make sure to check with you landlord or landlady first).

When getting a gun check all over to find one that feels right for you, and MAKE SURE TO GET TRAINED! If you set up a surveillance system make sure you have one on the front door and the back door, if you have an entrance to your basement on the outside of your house make sure to put one there and put one on each side of your house. Make sure that you can see all angles to make sure they can't get in.

Some People even go as far as finding a second location to keep some of their stockpile at, an undisclosed location that only they know about or ever visit in case something happens you still have something to fall back on. If you do this, make sure that you are the only one that knows about it. If the property is for sale if you can buy it. By owning the land you will be able to secure the area and build a shelter area so that the stockpile of food will last longer (even though it has a 5-25 year shelf life) keeping it in a dry area will make it last a little longer.

Now I just listed two ways you can protect it, there are other ways you can protect it's all up to how you want to do it, these are just examples of ways. Research a little and find out what fits your living situation the best. Remember when doing your own research, not everyone does the exact same thing so there is no wrong way to protect your stuff just as long as you do something to protect it.

Strategic Relocation
What it means and how to do it

What does Strategic Relocation mean? Strategic Relocation doesn't mean to pack up and move everything it means find different routes out of your town/city if something ever happens. When any disaster happens the roads are always jammed up because of traffic, you will not have to go through that if you know alternate routes out of your area. By knowing your routes can protect you from having car wrecks, running out of gas being stuck in a traffic jam, or being hijacked because your in a traffic jam.

For example, If you live in a densely populated area like New York City, Dallas Texas, Miami Florida, Hollywood California, or even Columbus Ohio just to name a few, you don't want to be stuck in the middle of everything. Travel around and look for alternate ways out, roads that don't get much traffic. Because if something goes down that you need to get out of the city you can without getting stuck in traffic.

Strategic Relocation can also mean coming up with a safe bug out location for government issues, such as

- Economic Collapse
- The Result of Gun Bans
- Martial Law
- Air borne Viruses causing city/county wide quarantine (make sure to have a face mask)

Having a second location (does not have to be a house/apartment or anything like that) is always a great thing in case the worst of the worst happens. When choosing a "bug out location" make sure that it a safe, sheltered (by trees) or can easily be sheltered with a little work on your end, and is away from the general public by a few miles. Don't let anyone know where this location is, and if you plan on staying there for long periods of time (over 72 hours) make sure to take some of your stockpile with you (enough to last your stay at this second location).

Knowing your area will help you greatly when picking a bug out spot. Knowing your surroundings at all times will keep you safer then you think when your finding your alternate routes to get out of your town, knowing when the streets are the busiest and when they are almost completely dead. Keeping all this in mind should make your venture into prepping for the worst easier then going into it blind eyed.

The Links

These are just a few of the links that you will find when doing your research on everything you need. These are the companies that I personally trust, they are reliable, cheaper then the rest, and have a great customer support team that actually cares about helping you with your personal journey.

Long Shelf Life Food (5-25 year shelf life)

Wise Food Storage – http://www.wisefoodstorage.com

Long Life Food - http://www.longlifefood.com

E-Foods Direct – http://www.efoodsdirect.com

Be Prepared – http://www.beprepared.com

First Aid Kits

First Aide Products - http://www.first-aid-product.com

Survival Unlimited – http://www.survivalunlimited.com

Hand Crank Generators

K-Tor – http://www.k-tor.com/pocket_socket.php

Solar Generators

My Solar Backup – http://www.mysolarbackup.com

Solar Blankets

Camping Survival - http://www.campingsurvival.com/emblan.html

I-Prepare - http://www.iprepare.com/100sh77ml.html

Hand/foot/body warmers

Hot Hands Direct - http://stn3.headgap.com/hothands/FMPro?-db=Ordershh.fp3&-format=products.htm&-new

Radio/Communication

Ambient Weather - http://www.ambientweather.com/emra.html

Be Prepared - https://beprepared.com/category.asp_Q_c_E_404_A_c2 c_E_ln_A_name_E_RadiosandCommunication

Tents

The Ready Store - http://www.thereadystore.com/2-person-tube-tent

Nitro Pak - http://www.nitro-pak.com/emergency-prep/shelter-supplies/tube-tent

Drinking Water

Life Straw - http://eartheasy.com/lifestraw-store-locations

Bug Out Bags

260 Tactical - http://www.260tactical.com/fox-tactical-duty-pack/

Camping Survival - http://www.campingsurvival.com/bugoutbafrbu.html

Storage For Your Stockpile

Global Industrial - http://www.globalindustrial.com/c/storage/bulk-rack/heavy-duty

Gilmore Kramer - http://www.gilmorekramer.com/more_info/ironman_22_gauge_open_steel_shelving/ironman_22_gauge_open_steel_shelving.shtml